Favourite
New Zealand JOKES
about Australians

Favourite New Zealand JOKES *about* Australians

Katrina Power

REED

Published by Reed Books, a division of Reed Publishing (NZ) Ltd, 39 Rawene Rd., Birkenhead, Auckland.
Associated companies, branches and representatives throughout the world.

ISBN 0 7900 0506 9

© 1996 Katrina Power

Illustrations by Geoff Hocking © The Five Mile Press Pty Ltd
Portions of this book were first published as
Favourite New Zealand Jokes About Australians

© 1992, 1996 Reed Publishing
This edition first published 1996
Reprinted 1997, 1999, 2000, 2001

The author asserts her moral rights in the work.

Designed by Clair Sutton
Printed in Australia by Griffin Press

DID YOU
HEAR THE ONE
ABOUT THE
KIWI ?

Introduction

Australians and New Zealanders have always given each other a hard time. Sibling rivalry is natural between two countries geographically close; between New Zealand and Australia it is particularly intense. Observe the crowd at any trans-Tasman sporting clash, and you will witness a rivalry that goes beyond the game itself. There is a difference in temperament too. New Zealanders see Australians as loud and uncouth, while Australians think of New Zealanders as slow and provincial.

One way in which the two peoples express their rivalry is in the telling of jokes at each other's expense. Some have been around for years, while others pass in and out of fashion quickly. Many are unprintable (!), but the selection offered here gives a fair idea of how Kiwis view their neighbours 'across the ditch'. When it comes to the crunch, however, Aussies and Kiwis are mates and can take a bit of good-natured ribbing.

The Australian cartoonist Stanley Cross once said: 'To create a good joke, you first have to have a good laugh and then think backwards.' He must have been talking about Australians when he said this.

'Dear Abby, I am a sailor in the navy. My parents live in Auckland, next door to my sister, who is a prostitute, and her husband, who is an Aussie drug smuggler. My brother is doing life in prison for murder. I am in love with a beautiful woman. She is a Jamaican prostitute who works the docks, and we intend to marry as soon as my VD clears up. When I leave the navy, we hope to set up a whore house in town, and ask my sister to work with us to keep it in the family. Although she knows nothing of my family background, I know that she won't have a problem with any of it, except for one thing — should I tell her my brother-in-law is an Australian?'

Aussie foreplay: 'Hey, you awake?'

You can tell an Aussie a mile off, but when he gets up close, you can't tell him a damn thing!

An Irishman built a long pier in the middle of the Nullarbor Plain — right slap bang in the middle of the desert. All the local people turned out to laugh at him.

'Only an Irishman would build a pier in the desert!' they jeered.
'Ah yes,' he replied, jingling the coins in his pocket and pointing to the figure sitting at the far end of the pier, 'but only an Australian would pay to be allowed to fish off the end of it!'

THEY'RE not all that flash in the outback — not too many modcons. One night Bruce and Blue were in the pub and won a weekend for two to Sydney in a raffle. So on Saturday night, there they were, tucked up in bed after a hard night's boozing, when Blue says, 'Bruce, I don't feel too good. Can you go downstairs and get me a glass of water?' So off Bruce trots, and when he returns, Blue drinks the lot and feels much better. An hour later he's awake again, and asks Bruce to help him out once more. This goes on most of the night, until Bruce comes back to bed about 6 am, empty handed. 'Where's me flaming drink?' demands Bruce. 'Look, mate, I'm really sorry, but when I went down this time, some bastard was sitting on the little porcelain well.'

How can you tell when Aussies are on the level?
They dribble out of *both* sides of their mouth.

Why do Australian horses run so fast?
They've seen what's happened to the sheep.

Why was the Christ child not born in Australia?
You'd have a job finding three wise men, much less a virgin!

What should you throw to a drowning Australian?
His wife and family.

NEWSFLASH! Bob Hawke's library burned down at the weekend
— and both books were destroyed! The real tragedy was that he
hadn't finished colouring in one of them.

Why don't Aussies take their girlfriends to the football?
They keep jumping the fence and eating the grass.

What's the difference between Aussies and pigs?
Pigs don't turn into Aussies when they drink.

What do you call an Aussie who farms both sheep
and goats?
Bisexual.

Why do Aussie men always make love with their
eyes closed?
They hate to see women enjoying themselves.

Bruce and Sheila were the proud parents of a healthy baby, and Bruce shouted the whole pub in celebration. 'What was your nipper, Bruce?' asked one of his mates. 'A little boy?' 'Nah, mate,' said Bruce, 'have another guess!'

Bruce's favourite breakfast was brains, but Sheila couldn't stomach the thought of eating something that came out of an animal's head. She'd much rather have an egg.

Bruce's mates thought he deserved to get into the Guinness Book of World Records for completing a 16-piece jigsaw in just 3 hours: it said on the box 3-4 years.

What does an Australian girl use for
protection during sex?
A bus shelter.

Why do Aussies marry women?
Sheep can't cook.

Aussies aren't too hot on science; they think the four seasons are
salt, pepper, vinegar and mustard.

Bruce's hobby is reading the obituaries, because he thinks it's
amazing that people manage to die in alphabetical order.

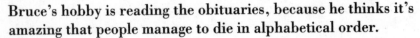

Four men (a Cuban, a Scot, a New Zealander and an Australian) were travelling across the Sahara Desert by train, and were discussing the various merits of the countries to pass the time.

The Cuban leaned back in his seat and took an enormous Havana cigar from his shirt pocket. He tipped the cigar, lit it, puffed on it once or twice, then threw it out of the window.

'What are you doing, man!' cried the others. 'Havana cigars are the best in the world!'

The Cuban waved his hands disparagingly. 'This stuff is like shit in my country,' he said. 'We have plenty of it.'

The Scot, not to be outdone, opened his suitcase and took out a bottle of Scotch, screwed off the lid, took two swigs and then threw it out the window.

'Hey!' the others cried. 'What are you doing? That's the best whisky available!'

'Och,' the Scot replied, 'this? It's like shit in my country — we have plenty of it.' 'Well,' thought the New Zealander,

'What am I going to do?'
Then he picked up the Aussie and threw him out the window.

A Kiwi and an Aussie were flying across the Tasman together. The smooth Kiwi decided to flirt with the flight attendant, so he called to her as she passed: 'Tickle your arse with a feather.'

'I beg your pardon!' she hissed,
as he looked innocently up at
her.
'I said,' he replied,
'Particularly nasty weather.'
'Oh,' she said. 'Yes.'
The Aussie decided that he would like to
try this trick himself, so called out to the next
attendant who passed;
'Stick a feather up your arse.'
'I beg your pardon! she exclaimed, as the Aussie smiled up at her.
'I said,' he replied, 'Bastard of a day, innit?'

Bruce went into the bank to withdraw a large sum of money. 'Can you identify yourself?' asked the teller. Bruce pulled a mirror from his pocket, peered into it and said, 'Yep, that's me all right.'

Do you know how many people work in the Australian Parliament? About half of them.

Bruce thought that the most ignorant people in the world lived in Tokyo — because the encyclopedia said that's where the population is the densest.

What's the difference between an Australian and a computer? You only have to punch information into a computer once.

DON'T LIKE THE SOFTWARE MUCH.

— OOF!

16

Bruce gave up tapdancing because he kept falling into the sink.

A simple Australian country girl was very surprised to be delivered of a baby.

'But you must have noticed that you were pregnant!' exclaimed the doctor.

'No,' she replied. 'My friends told me that I'd been bitten by the one-eyed trouser snake, and that it would take about nine months for the swelling to go down!'

A man found a koala wandering about Sydney by himself.

He approached a policeman and asked what he should do with the koala, as he really shouldn't be wandering the streets by himself.

'Take him to the zoo,' the policeman told the man. The next day he saw the same man with the koala walking down the street again. 'I thought I told you to take that koala to the zoo!' he said. 'I did,' said the man. 'And he liked it so much that today we thought we'd try a movie.'

Bruce's sister gave birth to twins, and the delighted uncle rushed off to register the births at the Town Hall. 'What have they called the babies, love, and what did they weigh?' asked the woman behind the counter. '8 pounds, 6 ounces, and that's Denise,' said Bruce. 'What a lovely name,' cooed the woman, 'and the other little tyke?' 'Eight pounds, ten,' said Bruce, 'and that's Denephew.'

Aussie tourists were taking in the sights of Madame Tussauds. An attendant approached their group and pointed to a woman who was standing stock still, staring at some of the really grotesque exhibits.

'Excuse me, sir, is that lady with your party?'

'Yes,' said Blue. 'That's my sister-in-law.'

'Well, please keep her moving,' said the attendant. 'We're stock-taking.'

The Aussies have invented a new type of parachute. It opens on impact.

Bruce and Blue were on the run from the law, and raced into a garden and hid up two trees. The police were hot on their heels with dogs snarling at the base of the first tree very soon after. 'Who's up there!' demanded a copper, and the quick-thinking Bruce called out 'Miaow.' 'It's just a cat, Sarge,' said the young copper as he moved to the second tree. 'Who's up there!' he demanded. 'Another cat!' replied Blue.

There's a Japanese firm that has developed a camera with a shutter speed so fast it can actually catch an Aussie with his mouth shut!

Bruce was being interviewed to become a police officer, and was given a general knowledge test. The senior constable chose three questions; 'Who,' he asked 'is our current Prime Minister?'

'Pass,' replied Bruce. 'Okay, this one's a bit easier,' said the officer. 'In which state is the Sydney Harbour Bridge?' 'Pass,' replied Bruce again. 'Good grief,' said the officer. 'Well, who killed Jesus Christ?' 'Pass,' replied Bruce once again. 'I strongly suggest,' said the officer, 'that you leave here and don't bother coming back until you find out!'

'How did the interview go, darling?' asked Bruce's mother. 'Did you get the job?' 'GET it,' snorted Bruce, 'I'm on a homicide case already!'

What's the worst thing about Australia?
It's above sea-level.

21

Why do birds fly upside down over Australia?
It's not worth shitting on.

The only way most Aussies would end up having 500 men under them is if they worked in a cemetery.

Bruce isn't sure how fast light travels, but one thing's for sure, it gets here too early in the morning!

Why can't you give an Aussie more than ten minutes for lunch?
If you did, you'd have to retrain him.

Two Aussies were walking down the
road. One said, 'Look! A dead bird!'
The other one looked up and
said, 'Where?'

Young Wayne was the star of a country high school's rugby team,
and had been training hard for the interprovincial high school
championship. Then, one morning assembly, the school principal
made a devastating announcement. 'As you know, Wayne Budd is
this school's greatest athlete, and, as such, we are all naturally
proud of him. However, it is the view of the school that we must
not neglect academic matters in favour of sporting prowess.

Wayne has not been successful in mathematics this year, so I am forced to withdraw him from the competition.' There was a stunned silence, as hopes of winning the championship crumbled, then a lone voice called 'Give him another chance!'

The cry was taken up by the crowd, and soon one hundred voices were calling 'Give him another chance! Give him another chance!' The principal was touched by the pleading from the crowd. 'Wayne Budd, come to the front of the hall,' he said. 'Wayne. What is 5 plus 5?' Wayne bit his lip and thought — and thought. '10?' he ventured. There was a moment's silence, then the entire crowd called out 'Give him another chance!'

The great Aussie gamehunter was stalking the jungles of Africa, looking for lions and tigers to shoot, when he stumbled across a beautiful woman, lying naked in a clearing.

'Wow!' he said, 'Are you game?'

She gave a seductive smile and said, 'Why, yes, I am!'
So he shot her.

You really shouldn't be out in the desert unless your vehicle is
reliable — and this one wasn't. There they were, two blokes and a
sheila, in a broken down ute, in the middle of the Australian
desert. 'Well,' sighed Bruce, 'I guess we'd better hop out and start
walking, see if we can get picked up, or find a billabong, or something.' 'Right,', said Sheila, who had all the common sense of the
three, 'Let's just grab one thing each to take with us. I'll take an
umbrella, so I can shelter from the sun, and catch any water if it
rains.' 'Okay,' said Bruce, 'I'll take the car seat, so we can sit
down if we get tired. What are you taking, Blue?' 'I'm taking the
car door,' said Blue, 'so I can wind the window down if it gets
too hot.'

An Aussie had been stranded
on a desert island for three years,
with nothing to eat but coconuts
when one day a beautiful
woman stepped on to the
beach from the surf, wearing
a skin-tight wetsuit.
'Man,' she said, 'Do you
hunger?'
'Yes,' he said, 'Yes, I
do!'
So the woman
unzipped a pocket on
the thigh of her suit
and brought out some
delicious food, which the Aussie ate, and was satisfied.
'Man,' said the woman again, 'Do you thirst?'

'Yes,' he replied, 'Yes, I do!' And the woman unzipped a pocket on the other thigh of the wetsuit, and took out a bottle of wine, which the Aussie drank, and was satisfied.

'Man,' said the woman, beginning to undo the zipper that led from her throat to her breasts, 'Do you want to play around?'

'My God,' said the Aussie, 'You mean you've got a set of golf clubs down there too!'

What's the difference between the Aussie cricket team and the Auckland Harbour Bridge?

You can't walk over the Harbour Bridge.

What does the Loch Ness monster have in common with an intelligent, sensitive Aussie? Some people believe they exist, but no one's actually seen either.

Why won't an Aussie drive a BMW?
He can't spell it.

Why don't Aussies like making Milo?
They can't figure out how to get eight cups of water into that little packet.

Bruce was approached by Jehovah's Witnesses, but didn't want anything to do with them. He couldn't — he hadn't even seen the accident.

What should you do if an Aussie throws a grenade at you?
Pull the pin and throw it back.

An Aussie and two of his Kiwi mates were fishing from a cliff, when one of them hauled up an old bottle on the end of his line. When he pulled it off the line, he gave it a quick wipe, and suddenly, a genie appeared in a swirling cloud of blue smoke. 'Thank you for releasing me from the ancient curse,' he growled, 'I will grant you one boon. Leap from the top of this cliff, call the name of whatever you desire, and you will land safely in a boat at the bottom, in a bountiful pile of that which you named.' And with that, he vanished in another puff of smoke. The first Kiwi thought for a while, then leapt off the cliff, calling 'Gold!' as he leapt, and landed in a dinghy, which was brimming with gold sovereigns. 'Diamonds!' yelled the second Kiwi, as he flung himself from the clifftop, before landing in a glittering boatload of sparkling gems. And the Aussie? Well, he just didn't think. The excitement was too much for him. As he jumped off the cliff, he yelled 'Whee!'

Why do Aussies have TGIF on the tops of their shoes?
So they know the toes go in first.

What do you call a field full of Australians?
A vacant lot.

What's the smallest room in Australia?
The Australian Hall of Fame.

Did you hear about the Aussie
who wanted to be buried at sea?
Six of his mates were drowned
trying to dig a hole.

A shearing gang — a Jew, a Hindu and an Aussie — drove into a small town and tried to book rooms at the hotel. 'I'm sorry, guys,' said the publican, 'but we're completely full. Two of you can share a room, but one of you will have to sleep in the barn with the animals.' 'No problem,' said the Jew, 'I'll sleep there, and catch up with you in the morning.' He left the room, but was back in the pub in a few minutes. 'Look, I can't spend the night in the barn,' he said, 'because there's a pig in there, and it's against my religion to have anything to do with such an unclean animal.' 'That's okay,' said the Hindu. 'I'll spend the night out there, and see you in the morning.' And off he went, only to come back into the pub within a few minutes. 'I'm sorry, guys,' he said, 'but I can't spend the night with a cow. We hold them sacred.' 'I don't mind,' said the Aussie, and he left to go and get settled for the night. A few minutes later the cow and the pig turn up at the door, saying, 'I'm sorry, there's no way we can sleep in the barn; there's an Aussie in there!'

How does an Aussie turn on the
light after having sex?
She opens the car door.

Bruce was chatting to the pretty
blonde assistant while he waited
for the butcher to fulfil his order. 'So, what time do you finish
work tonight?' he asked, '6 o'clock,' she replied. 'How about
having a drink with me?' 'I can't, I'm married,' she said. 'What
would my husband have to say?' 'Just tell him you've got a date,'
said Bruce. 'Tell him yourself,' she said. 'That's him out the back,
sharpening his knives.'

How many Aussies does it take to make chocolate chip cookies?
Ten. One to make the batter, and nine to peel the smarties.

'Bruce!' said Blue. 'I've just found out that your missus has been sleeping with Bill down the road and charging him $5 a go!' 'Well, the joke's on him,' said Bruce, 'because I've been sleeping with her for years, for FREE!'

Did you hear about the Australian abortion clinic?
There's a twelve month waiting list.

Sheila died and Bruce, in a rare, sensitive moment, decided to put a notice in the paper. 'Sheila died,' it read. 'Look, mate,' said the newspaperman, 'you can say more than that. You get a total of 6 free words for a death notice.' So Bruce changed the wording to read 'Sheila died. Tractor for sale.'

But Bruce wasn't cut out for a life without a woman, and was very lonely. He placed another notice in the paper. 'Woman wanted for companionship. Must be good looking, able to cook, clean and have own boat. Send picture of boat.'

How do you drive an Aussie crazy?
Give him a packet of M&Ms and tell him to put them in alphabetical order.

There are no dress codes in Australian bars — just a sign at the door saying 'Knuckles must not drag on the floor.'

The Texan visiting Australia was saying that everything to be found in America was bigger and better than anything found in Australia.
Just then a kangaroo hopped by.
'What the hell was that?' gasped the Texan.
'That?' said the Aussie casually.
'Just a grasshopper.'

BOOOING!

They'd made it to Atlanta to cheer their teams on at the Olympics, but the arena was too full, and they were denied entry. Quick as a wink, they came up with a plan to pose as athletes, and be admitted through the competitors' gate. Davey picked up a stick, rubbed the end of it to a point, and announced at the gate that he was 'Davey Green for England, javelin'. Mike pulled a hubcap off a car and called himself 'Michael O'Toole for Ireland, discus'. But who could compare with Bruce, who turned up with a roll of barbed wire and some nails and announced he was 'Bruce Clarke for Australia, fencing'.

'What's in the bag?' asked Bruce.
'Chickens,' was the reply.
'If I guess how many are in the bag, will you give me one?'
'Hey, if you guess how many are in the bag, I'll give you them both!' said Blue.
'Okay,' said Bruce, 'um . . . five!'

An Aussie walked into a bar with a large crocodile at the end of a chain.

'Do you serve Poms?' the Aussie asked the barman.

'Yes, sir, we serve English people,' the barman replied.

'Good. I'll have a pint of Fosters for me and three Poms for the croc.'

How can you tell if a step-ladder is made in Australia?
It has a sign at the top saying 'Stop here.'

A little Aussie boy got lost at a circus, so went up to a policeman and said,
'I've lost my dad.'
'Have you, mate?' said the policeman. 'What's he like?'
'Beer and women,' said the boy.

How can you tell when an Aussie's been in your freezer?
There are love bites on the leg of lamb.

An Australian couple were taking a world cruise for their honeymoon. The first evening on board, they received a note in their cabin asking them to sit at the Captain's table for dinner that night.

'I can't believe it!' said the bridegroom. 'We paid all that money for this cruise, and we still have to eat with the crew!'

It was their first big plane trip, and Bruce and Blue were headed overseas to Bali. They were due to land in about an hour, when the pilot made an announcement. 'Good afternoon, ladies and gentlemen. As you may be aware, we are roughly an hour from Bali, but have unfortunately lost one of our four engines, and so will now arrive half an hour later than scheduled. There's no cause for alarm, so just sit back and enjoy the flight.'

Fifteen minutes later the pilot made another announcement; 'Ladies and gentlemen, we have lost a second engine, but I repeat: there is absolutely NO cause for alarm, however, we are now an hour behind the time originally scheduled to arrive in Bali.'

Ten more minutes passed before the pilot, this time sounding a little nervous, announced 'Ladies and gentlemen, we have lost a third engine. Although we will now be arriving in Bali two hours behind schedule, I repeat: there is NO cause for alarm, please enjoy the flight, but remain in your seat, with seat belts fastened.'

'Hell's bells!' said Bruce, who had been paying close attention to events,

'I hope we don't lose that last bloody engine.
We'll be up here all day!'

What do you call an Aussie who
marries an Irishman?
A social climber.

Walking the streets of Bali, a street vendor sidled up to Bruce. 'Hello, sir, I have first class pornographic material, with beautiful girls . . . Very cheap!' 'It's no use,' Bruce said sadly, 'we haven't got a pornograph.'

An Australian couple won a million dollars in Lotto. Although they were both thrilled, the wife had one concern.
'What about all the begging letters, honey? she asked her husband.
'Just keep sending them,' he replied.

Still travelling through Bali, Bruce and Blue decided to split up and do a bit of exploring. When they met up later that evening, Bruce was driving a gleaming white Porsche. 'Wow!' said Blue, 'where'd you get that?' 'Well,' said Bruce, 'I was walking through the town, having a bit of look round, when this car pulled up, and this gorgeous blonde offered to show me the countryside.

We drove for a bit, and then we pulled over to a secluded spot, and she took a picnic basket from the back of the car, and we had a fabulous lunch. Then she took off all her clothes, lay back on the blanket and told me to take whatever I wanted. So I took the car.'

'Too right!' said Blue. 'You'd look bloody silly in her clothes!'

'Blue, I'm pregnant,' Raelene told her boyfriend.
'And if you don't marry me, I'm going to throw myself off the Harbour Bridge!'
'Raelene, you're amazing,' said Blue. 'Not only are you great in bed, but you're a good sport too.'

43

They were watching a game of cricket between New Zealand and Australia, and things were getting pretty heated in the terraces, with supporters from both sides screaming insults and throwing beer cans at each other. Bruce was so nervous that he couldn't enjoy the game, and kept looking over his shoulder. 'Look, mate,' said Blue, 'why worry about it until something happens? After all, if one of those cans has your name on it . . .' 'Oh, great!' replied Bruce. 'My name's Foster!'

An Australian town council were voting on how much money to put aside to build a public urinal. They decided to double the sum, and to build an arsenal as well.

Grandma came over from New Zealand to stay while Bruce and Sheila went off on a bit of a holiday. She was shocked by the children's manners, and in particular, by their language. 'Right!' she thought, 'I'm going to be tough on these kids. It's for their own good.' The next morning, at breakfast, she said to Wayne, 'Good morning sweetheart, what would you like to eat this morning?' 'I'll have some of them bloody cornflakes,' said Wayne, and was completely surprised when Grandma belted him around the ears. 'And what about you, darling?' Grandma asked Darlene. She replied, 'I dunno, Grandma, but it won't be none of them bloody cornflakes!'

Sheila phoned Doris for a gossip — 'I heard Bruce was admitted to hospital last night with 12 stabs wounds to the head!' Sheila replied 'Well, he's not used to eating with a fork, but he's getting a lot better!'

What do you call an Aussie who scores well in an IQ test?
A cheat.

What are the best four years of an Aussie's life?
Fifth form.

Bruce and Blue started a job as truck drivers and were rumbling down the highway in a rig, when the road passed under a bridge next to a large sign — Height clearance 11' 13'. 'We can't go under there, Blue,' said Bruce. 'Our truck is 12' 6'.'
'Why don't we just nip on under?' asked Blue. 'I can't see any cops around.'

In a court case the other day there was this poor, distressed Aussie girl who didn't even know she'd been raped — until the cheque bounced!

Why don't Aussies look out of the window in the morning at work? Because then they'd have nothing to do in the afternoon.

The manager of the hotel chain decided to do a spot of quality control, so checked into one of his hotels incognito. He inspected his room thoroughly, making sure that everything was clean, tidy and comfortable, before heading down to the bar. He was pleased with the drink he was served, and with the music and ambience in the bar. He moved through into the restaurant, and was served by Bruce. Throwing his menu aside, he asked Bruce to choose something for him to eat, and was very pleased with Bruce's choice.

After the meal, he complimented Bruce on the meal and the service, and told Bruce who he was. Bruce whispered discreetly in his ear. 'Any time you want a decent feed, you come on in here and ask old Bruce — I don't care that you can't read!'

What's the difference between yoghurt and Australians?
At least yoghurt has a little culture.

Bruce was travelling through Germany, when he made the acquaintance of a pretty German lass. She invited him home, and they made passionate love all night long. The following morning she cooked him an enormous breakfast, and Bruce was overwhelmed by the wonderful hospitality. 'Can I give you some money to show my appreciation?' he asked, holding out some dollar bills. 'Forget the dollars,' she said, 'how about marks?' 'You got it,' said Bruce, 'Honey, you get 10 out of 10!'

A man came into Bruce's barber shop and enquired how long it would be before Bruce was free. 'An hour,' replied Bruce, and the man said that he'd come back later. He didn't return until the following day, when he asked the same question, and was told 'an hour and a half' this time, before he disappeared again. This went on for a week, until Bruce was so curious that he sent his assistant to follow the man, and find out where he went. The assistant was back within a couple of minutes and reported, 'he nips around to your place!'

Did you know that New Zealanders who emigrate to Australia raise the IQ of both countries?

Did you hear about the Aussie who had a brain transplant?
The brain rejected him a week later.

Why did the Aussies stop making ice?
Because the old lady who knew the recipe died.

I'm outa here!

Twenty percent of Australian teenagers don't know what premarital intercourse is. Ten percent have never indulged in it.

Bruce snored loudly — so loudly that Sheila would say 'I swear, Bruce, one day you'll snore your guts up!' This went on for years, until one day, Sheila couldn't take it any more. She went to the butcher's that afternoon and bought a sheep's heart, some chicken livers and some pigs' kidneys, and that night, while Bruce was sleeping, arranged them around Bruce's head on his pillow. The next morning Bruce stumbled down to breakfast, ashen-faced. 'Why Bruce,' asked Sheila, 'whatever is the matter?' 'You're not going to believe this, Sheila! I always thought you were winding me up, but no! You were right! This morning I woke up to find that I'd snored all me guts up!' 'No!' said Sheila. 'Let's get you to a hospital!' 'No, I'm okay now,' he said. 'By the grace of God, and with the aid of a toothbrush, I got them all back down.'

Sheila went to her father in great distress. 'Dad, I'm pregnant,' she said.

'Hang on a minute,' said he. 'Are you sure it's yours?'

The American tourist was bragging again, this time about how efficient builders were. 'The Statue of Liberty was put together in only 6 weeks,' he claimed. 'Hah! That's nothing!' laughed the Frenchman. 'The Eiffel Tower was raised in only one month! And you, little Australian, what's that bridge — how long did that take to build?' 'That?' asked Bruce, pointing at the Sydney Harbour Bridge, 'Dunno what that is. Wasn't there yesterday.'

Australian outback has two main industries: crocodiles and tourists, and they skin them both.

Blue and Sheila were sitting together on the couch. He was watching TV, she was reading their horoscopes. Suddenly she turned to Blue and slapped his face.

'That,' she shouted, 'is for next week!'

I went to a concert by Yehudi Menuhin with my Aussie mate last week.

He leaned over and whispered 'What's he playing?'

I replied, 'Chaconne in D.'

He looked at me blankly.

I said, 'A violin.'

Bruce and Blue stagger into a bar in Sydney where they proceed to celebrate Blue's birthday in style. 'This one's on me, Bruce!' slurs Blue, as he tosses a couple of bottle tops onto the bar. 'Hey, what's this!' demands the barman, but Bruce takes him aside. 'Look, mate, it's his birthday, and he's not very bright. He thinks he's shouting me a good time tonight, so just play along with it, and I'll fix you up at the end of the night before we head off.' The barman agrees, and Bruce and Blue party up a storm, singing along with the music, and Blue being very generous with his bottle tops, buying Bruce anything he likes to drink. Finally, as they're about to stagger out into the night, the barman calls to Bruce, 'Hey! Don't forget you've got to settle up your bill!' 'Yeah, right!' says Bruce, 'I nearly forgot. How much do we owe you?' 'Close to three hundred bucks,' is the reply. 'Well,' says Bruce, 'I haven't got anything small on me. Have you got change for a manhole cover?'

How many Aussie blokes does it take to
change a light-bulb?
None, that's women's work.

A traveller walked into the pub with a
mangy old dog and a kookaburra, and a
tatty old banjo. He sat back and sipped
his beer whilst the dog began to strum the banjo, and the kookaburra danced on the tabletops and sang. Bruce and Blue were
amazed. They dropped some coins into the traveller's hat, and sat
back and really enjoyed the show. At the end of the night they
walked up to the traveller and congratulated him on the act. 'You
could be a big name!' cried Bruce, 'you could make it on telly!'
'Nah!' replied the traveller. 'I'll let you guys in on a secret. The
kookaburra can't sing a note — the dog's a ventriloquist!'

An Aussie was down at the pub having a quiet drink, when the barman told him a riddle.

'My mother had a child, but it wasn't my brother or my sister. Who was it?'

The Aussie thought about it for a while, but couldn't come up with the answer.

'I give up,' he said.

'It was me! said the barman.

Blue thought this was quite a good riddle, so he tried it on his wife when he got home. But she couldn't come up with the answer either.

'I give up,' she said. 'Who was it?'

'The barman from the Oak and Whale!' he replied.

There's an Aussie guy who has this terrific line when he's out with a girl. He drives her out to a deserted, moonlit spot and says he wants to talk about the hereafter.

She's usually interested until he says 'If you're not here after what I'm here after, you'll be here after I'm gone!'

Amazing, the people you meet in pubs. Bruce was supping his usual Friday ale, when a man walked into the place, opened his rucksack and took out a little man, only a foot high, and a very small piano. He placed both of these on the bar, and the small man began to play beautiful music, which the locals rewarded with coins in the traveller's hat. Bruce, being curious, sidled up to the traveller to ask how he was fortunate enough to have encountered the little man. 'Well,' said the traveller. 'It's a funny story, actually. I was walking along the beach one day when I noticed a bottle which had been washed up by the tide. I opened it, and out spilled a genie. He was so happy to have been released that he gave me a wish. And here I am today, with a 12 inch pianist. How was I to know the genie was hard of hearing!'

What does an Aussie wear when he's formally dressed?
Black thongs.

How can you tell when a sick Aussie is getting better?
He tries to blow the froth off his medicine.

An Australian is someone who thinks that the three major political parties in Australia are Labor, Liberal and Cocktail.

An Englishman wanted to become an Irishman, so he visited a doctor to find out how to go about this.

'Well,' said the doctor, 'this is a very delicate operation, and there is a lot that can go wrong. I will have to remove half of your brain.'

'That's okay,' said the Englishman. 'I've always wanted to be Irish, and I'm prepared to take that risk.'

The following day, the operation went ahead, but the Englishman woke to find a look of horror on the face of the doctor.

'I'm so terribly sorry!' the doctor said. 'We've made the most awful mistake! Instead of removing half your brain, we've taken the whole brain out!'

The patient replied, 'She'll be right, mate! Chuck us a Fosters!'

Sheila decided to turn her back on the rough ways of men and embrace the life of the convent. One Saturday afternoon, on a convent outing at the zoo, the nuns passed too close to the cage of a ferocious gorilla and young Sister Sheila was dragged through the bars. All the nuns screamed and cried, but by the time poor Sister Sheila was rescued from the cage of the amorous gorilla, she had been most thoroughly ravaged and was in a comatose state. She was rushed to hospital and was found to be largely unhurt, but was kept in hospital for observation as she was clearly distraught, and refused to talk to anyone. After 14 days the mother superior decided that she would try to approach Sister Sheila, and tiptoed into the ward. 'Sister Sheila,' she called softly, 'would it help if you talked about it? Have you recovered from that animal's attentions?'

'Recovered!' cried poor heartbroken Sister Sheila. 'He's a beast! Two weeks it's been, and not a letter, not a phone call . . .'

Did you hear about the Aussie who bought a new pair of jandals but took them back the next day, wanting a longer piece of string?

What do you call 500 Australians at the bottom of the sea?
A start.

What do you have when an Australian is up to his neck in concrete?
Not enough concrete.

What do you call an Australian standing in the middle of a paddock?
A thicket.

Two Aussies were stranded on an iceberg.
'Look Blue,' said one, 'we're saved.
Here comes the *Titanic*.'

An Englishman, a New Zealander and an Australian were discussing their wives and families while on a long trip.

'I have a beautiful wife,' said the Englishman. 'And we have 10 beautiful children, all boys. One more and I'd have a cricket team.'

'My wife is fabulous,' said the Kiwi. 'A great cook, and we have 14 great kids, all boys as well. One more and we'd have a rugby team.'

The two men turned expectantly to the Aussie and asked, 'Well, mate? What about you?'

'I don't have any kids,' the Aussie said sadly. 'But I've got 17 terrific wives. One more and I'd have a golf course!'

The Aussie Water Polo team would have done better in the finals had three of its horses not drowned.

Sheila was burying Bruce, and gave him one last, loving look as he lay in the open casket. 'Look at the stupid old bugger,' she said. 'He's smiling because he died in his sleep and doesn't know he's dead yet, and when he wakes up and finds out he's dead, the shock will kill him!'

Why did the Aussie woman cross the road?
Who cares? She shouldn't have been
out of the kitchen!

How many Aussies does it take to change a light-bulb?
What's a light-bulb?

How many Aussie men does it take to change a light bulb?
Only one — he holds onto the lightbulb and the world revolves around him.

Aussies always hang around in gangs so that they can form dope rings.

Blue to Bruce — 'I had a very difficult birth — I weighed only 4 pounds.'
'Four pounds!' exclaimed Bruce. 'Did you live?'
'Live!' said Blue. 'You should see me now!'

What do you call an Aussie with half a brain?
Gifted.

An Aussie is proof that God has a sense of humour.

HA! HA! HA! BEEWDY!

Young Wayne's teacher answered the telephone. 'Wayne has a very bad cold and can't come to school today,' said the voice. 'Is that so?' enquired Miss Johnson. 'And to whom am I speaking?'
'Oh, this is my father.'

An Aussie once won the Tour de France, but went missing immediately afterwards. They discovered him doing a lap of honour.

A Swiss bobsleigh team was competing in the Winter Olympics, but there was a terrible crash. The Swiss team met the Australian team coming up.

Blue was woken by the phone ringing in the middle of the night, so he got out of bed to answer it.

'Hello?' said the caller. 'Is this seven-five-double-two-double-two?'

'No' said Blue, 'this is seven-five-two-two-two-two.'

'Oh. Sorry to have disturbed you,' said the caller.

'That's okay,' said Blue. 'I had to get up anyway. The phone was ringing.'

Bruce and Blue were discussing wombats, when Sheila interrupted. 'If I find a womball, can I play too?'

What do you call a beautiful
woman in Australia?
A tourist.

If Santa Claus, a smart Aussie and a dumb blonde were in a room,
and you tossed in a hundred dollar note, who would grab it first?
The blonde — the other two don't exist.

Sheila was giving details of her car accident to the police.
'Speeding, officer? Oh no! Not me!' The policeman didn't believe a
word of it. 'Look, lady, what gear were you in?' 'A denim skirt, a
white shirt and a red jacket. What does that have to do with it!'

What's the difference
between an Aussie and
a bucket full of shit?
The bucket.

'Got a match, Bruce?'
'Nup, but I got a lighter.'
'Don't like lighters. Fluid
gets in me mouth when I'm
picking me teeth.'

When I went to get my IQ tested, I asked what the difference was between a high and a low IQ. They told me that with a high IQ of 170, a person could go to university, and that with a low IQ, someone might have trouble tying their shoelaces.
Ever notice that Aussies wear thongs?

Bruce is the only guy I know who can lose $100 on the FA Cup, and another $100 on the replay.

Blue is such a considerate bloke. He was watching the golf on telly, but he had the sound down really low, so as not to disturb Greg Norman when he was putting.

What's the difference between an Aussie and a Neanderthal? The Aussie didn't have the ambition to evolve that far.

Bruce and Sheila decided to adopt a Romanian baby, and put their application into the agency with very high hopes. Sure enough, a letter came the following week confirming that a 5 month old baby girl would be delivered to them within a fortnight. Bruce and Sheila were so excited that they rushed out to sign up for Romanian language classes, so that they would be able to understand their baby when she was old enough to talk.

Bruce had a part-time job cleaning the gorilla cage at the zoo. Then one day Bozo, the male gorilla, died, and Flora, his mate, was inconsolable and pined for him for weeks. In despair, the directors of the zoo approached Bruce with an unorthodox plan. 'Bruce,' they said, 'we've noticed that you're very fond of Flora, and we've got a plan which we think will cheer her up. For $1,000, would you sleep with her?' Bruce was confused. True, he was very fond of Flora, but he wasn't sure about the whole deal, so asked if he could think about it over the weekend.

When he came back to work on Monday, he sat down in the director's office and said that he'd reached a decision. 'You're right,' he said, 'I'm very fond of Flora, so I'll agree to your suggestion on three conditions. The first is that there'll be no kissing on the lips. The second is that any child of the union be brought up as a Catholic. The third is — can I pay you in instalments? It's going to take me a while to get $1,000 together.'

An Englishman, an Irishman, an Australian and a New Zealander were in a plane, getting ready to make their first parachute jump. The Englishman's exit was spectacular; he leapt out of the plane with the cry, 'I'm doing this for my country . . .'

The Irishman leapt out immediately afterwards, calling out the same words.

Then the New Zealander ripped the parachute off the Australian, pushed him out of the plane and cried, 'I'm doing this for my country!'

They were sitting by the fire with a steaming cup of coffee each, relaxing after a hard day's work. Blue's dog was licking his private parts, and Bruce watched him enviously. 'Y'know,' he said, 'I've always wanted to be able to do that.' 'Doesn't bother me,' said the ever-generous Blue, 'but I'd pat him a bit, first. He can be a bit vicious at times.'

How do you define 144 Australians?
Gross stupidity.

The Aussie pilot, when asked for
his height and position, replied,
'I'm 5'11' and sitting in the
front seat.'

Blue and Sheila were arguing about economising. 'If only you
could cook,' moaned the husband, 'we could sack the cook.'
'And if only you could make love properly,' said the wife,
'we could sack the gardener.'

An elephant had escaped from a circus and no trace had been found of it until Sheila, who had never seen an elephant before, rang the police in a terrible state.

'There's a horrible big monster in my garden,' she cried. 'It's pulling up my cabbages with its tail and then it's . . . it's . . . oh I can't describe what it's doing with them!'

Let's make love,' said
the Aussie.

'It won't take long, did it?'

An Aussie was accused of raping a girl, and was lined up in an identity parade. When the girl was brought into the police station to face the row of men, the Aussie pointed at her and said: 'That's her!'

'Why do Aussies call their beer XXXX?
Because they can't spell beer.

There were quite a bunch of them having a lads' night out at Kitty O'Brien's Irish Pub, and they were drinking up a storm. 'God Bless the Queen', was Bruce's first toast, followed quickly by 'God Bless President Clinton', 'Down with Hussein' and then 'Down with the Pope', when Paddy O'Brien up and belted Bruce one fair on the nose. When he came to, Blue asked him, 'You stupid fool, didn't you know Paddy was Irish?' 'Yeah, I did,' said Bruce, 'but no-one told me that the Pope was!'

How do you bring up a baby?
Stick your fingers down a dingo's throat.

What do you call a baby in a pram?
Meals on wheels.

The stockman started work on a station in the outback, and his first job was to check the fenceline, which, because the station was so huge, would take him two weeks to complete. He was half way around the property, when the owner of the station next door rode up to the fenceline to greet him. 'Gidday. You're that new fella from next door, aren't ya?' he asked, and when the stockman replied that he was, said 'look, if you're not doing anything on Friday, why don't you pop around? Things get pretty lonely out here, but I can guarantee all you can eat, as much as you can drink, great company and as much sex as you can handle.' 'Great,' said the stockman, 'who else will be there?' 'Just the two of us,' said the station owner.

The dingo was innocent!

How do you get an Aussie to laugh on a Monday?
Tell him a joke on Friday.

Bruce was filling out a census form. Length of residence in
Australia was, he wrote, 15 metres including the verandah and
front steps.

Bruce was doing his big OE, and was taking in the sights of
Jerusalem. When he returned to his hotel room, he and Blue
compared everything they'd seen and done that day. 'Y'know,
some guy in the market tried to sell me the skull of Jesus today.'
'No!', said Blue, 'you weren't fooled by that, were you?' 'Heck,

no!' replied Bruce. 'I told him that Stan next door already owns it, and he couldn't fool me.' 'So what's that, then?' asked Blue, poking around in Bruce's knapsack. 'That?' said Bruce, 'that's the skull of Jesus as a young child!'

A husband and wife were discussing what would happen if one of them were to die.

'Will you remarry, Blue? asked the wife.

'No, I don't think so,' said the husband.

'But I would want you to be happy, and to show you how sincere I am, she could have all my jewellery too!'

'Don't talk like that, darling,' he said.

'No, I mean it,' she said. 'Even tho' you don't have anyone in mind now, you will soon find someone to take my place. And when you do, you can also give her all my golf clubs.'

'No, that's no good, darling. She's left-handed.'

Most Aussies aren't too good at history. For example, they think Gandhi's first name was Goosey Goosey.

Young Sheila was a bit nervous about meeting the big boss at her first job interview, and was keen to impress. She looked nervously around the reception area as she sat and waited, and noticed a golf club and a couple of golf balls in the corner. Not being much of a cultured lass, she asked the woman on the front desk 'What are those?' and 'Golf balls,' was the reply. Once she was finally admitted to the interviewing room, she noticed an entire bucket of golf balls in the corner. 'My gosh!' she exclaimed, 'you must have killed one heck of a lot of golfs!'

They were drunk as skunks on their big OE, somewhere outside London, and were trying to stagger their way home. 'Dja have enny idea where we are, Bruce?' slurred Blue, as he stumbled around in the dark. 'Think it's a graveyard,' said Bruce, 'cause I've just smacked into a headstone. Lemme have a look . . .' he struck a match '. . . yep, and this guy's not such an old beggar, either. 50 — some guy called Miles from London.'

An Aussie was visiting a farm in New Zealand. After touring the property he turned to his host and bragged, 'Back home I could get into my car, drive all day, and by evening, not have reached the other side of my station!'
The Kiwi replied, 'You know, I had a car like that once too.'

How does an Aussie spell 'farm'?
EIEIO.

Bruce and Blue were playing golf one Saturday afternoon. Bruce was lining up a putt on the 9th hole, when a funeral procession drove past the golf course. Bruce straightened up, held his hand over his heart and stood in silence until the procession had passed. 'Heck, Bruce, I never knew you were so sensitive!' said Blue. 'That was real respect for the dead, that was!' Heck, it was nothing.' protested Bruce.
'How can one quiet moment compare with the 25 years she and I've had together?'

Why don't people want to play hide-and-seek with Australians? Because they don't ever want to find them.

What do you call an Australian with an IQ of 120?
Brisbane.

What is long and hard and stuffs Australians?
Primary school.

What do you get if you cross a sheep with an Australian?
Nothing. There are some things even sheep won't do.

The best three types of milkshake: thick, extra thick and
Australian.

What's the difference between an Aussie wedding and an Aussie funeral?
One less drunk.

What's the definition of optimism?
Australian batsmen wearing zinc on their faces during the World Cup.

An Englishman was walking through a sheep station in the outback when he came across an Australian sitting with his arms around a sheep. "Hey," he said, "shouldn't you be shearing that?" "Clear off!" said the Aussie. "Find your own!"

Three men had been sentenced to death by guillotine while travelling through a very religious country.

The first man placed his head on the block, the blade came crashing down — and stopped halfway.

'Praise be to Allah!' cried the watching crowd. 'The man is blessed, he shall not die!'

The second man placed his head on the block — and the same thing happened. The blade stuck halfway, and the crowd demanded his freedom.

The third man was an Aussie. As he placed his head on the block, he looked up and noticed that the blade was catching on a rusty bolt.

'Hey,' he said. 'Your problem's right here!'

Bruce and Sheila were out for a family drive, with three kids in the front and Sheila and the twins in the back, when Bruce was pulled over for speeding.

'Good afternoon, sir,' said the officer. 'Couldn't help but notice that you were speeding back there. Where are you off to in such a hurry?'

'What's that, dear?' called Sheila from the back.

'Says we were speeding,' said Bruce over his shoulder.

'I'm sorry, officer. We're going for a drive up to Ballarat to see the family, and I didn't notice the speed I was doing.'

'Ballarat!' exclaimed the officer. 'I went to school up there. Lovely old school by the river, big old trees to play on — those were the days!'

'What's that, dear?' called Sheila from the back.

'Says he knows Ballarat,' said Bruce.

'But,' continued the policeman. 'Ugly women! Boy, they were ugly! There was this one sheila who was so ugly that the flies

wouldn't touch her!'
'What's that, dear?' called Sheila from the back.
'Says he knows you.'

Sheila accompanied her husband to the doctor's office. After the checkup, the doctor took her aside and said, 'Your husband is suffering from severe long-term stress and it's affecting his cardiovascular system. He's a good candidate for either a heart attack or a stroke. If you don't do the following four things, your husband will surely die.

'First, each morning, fix him a healthy breakfast and send him off to work in a good mood.

'Second, at lunch time, make him a warm, nutritious meal and put him in a good frame of mind before he goes back to work.

'Third, for dinner, fix an especially nice meal, and don't burden him with household chores.

'Fourth, and most important for invigorating him and relieving stress, have sex with him several times a week and satisfy his every whim in bed.'

On the way home in the car, Bruce turned to Sheila and asked, 'So, I saw the doctor talking to you and he sure seemed serious. What did he tell you?'

'You're going to die,' she replied.